GENGHIS KHAN
and the Mongol Empire

by Miriam Greenblatt

BENCHMARK BOOKS

MARSHALL CAVENDISH
NEW YORK

ACKNOWLEDGMENT

With thanks to Dr. Morris Rossabi of the Department of East Asian Languages and Cultures, Columbia University, New York City, for his expert reading of the manuscript.

Benchmark Books
Marshall Cavendish Corporation
99 White Plains Road
Tarrytown, New York 10591-9001
Website: www.marshallcavendish.com

Library of Congress Cataloging-in-Publication Data
Greenblatt, Miriam.
Genghis Khan and the Mongol Empire / Miriam Greenblatt.
p. cm.—(Rulers and their times)
Includes bibliographical references and index.
Summary: Describes how Genghis Khan became the ruler of the Mongols and how these nomadic people lived.
ISBN 0-7614-1027-9 (lib. bdg.)
1. Genghis Khan, 1162–1227—Juvenile literature. 2. Mongols—Kings and rulers—Biography—Juvenile literature. 3. Mongols—Social life and customs—Juvenile literature. [1. Genghis Khan, 1162–1227. 2. Kings, queens, rulers, etc. 3. Mongols—Social life and customs.] I. Title. II. Series
DSS22 .G69   2001   950'2.—dc21   [B]   99-086634

Printed in Hong Kong
1 3 5 6 4 2

Picture Research by Linda Sykes Picture Research, Hilton Head SC
Cover: James Stanfield/ National Geographic Society Image Collection; pages 5, 6-7, 13, 69: Bibliotheque Nationale, Paris/AKG London; page 9: Topkapi Palace Museum, Istanbul/Bridgeman Art Library; page 10: Stapleton Collection/Bridgeman Art Library; pages 15, 22, 35: Bibliotheque Nationale, Paris/The Bridgeman Art Library; pages 18, 59: British Library/The Art Archive; pages 25, 62: Guliston Imperial Library, Teheran/Werner Forman Archive, Art Resource; page 26: Bibliotheque Nationale, Paris/AKG, Berlin/Superstock; page 28: The Metropolitan Museum of Art, Francis M. Weld Gift Fund, 1948 Photograph © The Metropolitan Museum of Art; pages 34, 37, 51: The Granger Collection; pages 38-39: Bibliotheque Nationale, Paris/ET Archive, London/Superstock; pages 41, 46: Dean Conger/Corbis; pages 43, 73: AKG London; pages 49, 56: Victoria and Albert Museum, London/Art Resource; page 53: Mansell Collection/TimePix; pages 64-65: Fogg Art Museum, Cambridge MA/Burstein Collection/Corbis

Permission has been granted to use extended quotations from the following copyrighted works:
———"How Storytelling Began Among the Mongol People" and "Why the Bat Lives in the Dark," from *Mongolian Folktales* by Hilary Roe Metternich, Avery Press, 1996, Boulder, Colorado. Reprinted by permission of the publisher.
———*The Khan's Daughter: A Mongolian Folktale* by Laurence Yep. Published by Scholastic Press, a division of Scholastic Inc. Copyright © 1997 by Laurence Yep. Reprinted by permission of Scholastic Inc.
———*The Secret History of the Mongols: The Origin of Chinghus Khan* by Paul Kahn, North Point Press, 1984. Copyright © 1984 Paul Kahn. Reprinted by permission of the author.

Contents

The Great Khan

Many different people have affected the course of history. There have been religious leaders like Gautama Buddha, political leaders like Mohandas Gandhi, men of science like Albert Einstein, and inventors like Thomas A. Edison. Perhaps the greatest military genius the world has ever known was the son of a herder from the grasslands of east-central Asia. His name was Genghis Khan, and under his leadership Mongol horsemen conquered an empire that stretched from the Pacific Ocean all the way to the Caspian Sea. Under his descendants, the Mongol Empire expanded to include most of Russia, China, and eastern Europe. It was the largest land empire the world has ever seen.

Even Christopher Columbus's voyages to the Americas owe something to Genghis Khan. When Columbus sailed across the Atlantic, he carried letters addressed to the Mongol emperor, as well as a book by Marco Polo in which the Venetian described his travels through the Mongol Empire.

In this book, you will read how Genghis Khan rose from poverty and obscurity to become a mighty ruler. You will learn how the people in a nomadic society lived—the clothes they wore and the foods they ate, as well as the houses, sports, and arts they carried with them from place to place. Finally, you will read some folktales and sayings in which the Mongols tell us about themselves in their own words.

Between 1921 and 1990, when Mongolia was under the rule of the Soviet Union, Genghis Khan was considered a tyrant who was best forgotten. Since Mongolia regained its freedom, he is once again looked upon as a national hero.

PART ONE

The Persians produced many manuscripts about Genghis Khan's conquest of their country. Illustrations such as this show Mongol warriors in action.

Empire

Early Years

The conqueror known to history as Genghis Khan was born around 1167. Legend has it that he came into the world clutching a large blood clot in his right fist, a sure sign that he would grow up to become a great and successful warrior. His father, Yisugei the Brave, named his newborn son Temuchin, after an enemy chief whom Yisugei had just captured.

Temuchin spent his childhood in his father's camp along the Onon River in Mongolia. Like all Mongol children, he learned to ride horseback as soon as he could walk. In summer, he practiced archery by shooting at birds. In winter, he played on the frozen river. His closest companion was a boy from another tribe named Jamuka. Temuchin and Jamuka were so close, in fact, that they became blood brothers. They gave each other knucklebones and handmade arrows, and swore eternal friendship.

Becoming a blood brother meant that if Temuchin's clan (a group of related families) were attacked, Jamuka would come to its defense. If Jamuka's tribe had its animals stolen, Temuchin would help the tribe recover its property.

When Temuchin was about nine years old, Yisugei set off with his son to find him a fiancée. Marriage was a good way to form an alliance with another tribe and, if possible, increase the wealth and prestige of one's family. Yisugei sought a match among a tribe called the Onggirat. He found his son's future bride in a ten-year-old girl named Borte, who possessed not only a pretty face and flashing eyes but also a valuable dowry: a cloak of rare black sable. As was customary, Temuchin was left to live with his future parents-in-law for one year.

On his way home, Yisugei came across some Tartars camped on the plain. Since it was the practice for nomads to offer hospitality to strangers, the Tartars invited Yisugei to join them in their meal. Unfortunately for Yisugei, the Tartars had recognized him as an enemy who had robbed them in the past, and they put poison in his food. Yisugei managed to reach his camp, but realizing that he

For a people who moved from place to place finding fresh pasture for their cattle, no animal was more important than the horse. The horse controlled the Mongols' herds, provided transportation, and helped defend against attack. Here, a Mongol nomad is pictured watching his horse drink water.

Tartars at camp. The Tartars were probably the richest of Mongolia's tribes. Their grazing lands contained large deposits of silver, which they used for making dishes and tools.

would soon die, he sent a messenger to bring Temuchin home. By the time Temuchin returned, his father was dead. Shortly after, the soldiers who had served under Yisugei rode off to join another tribe, the Tayichi'ut. Temuchin and his family were left alone.

For the next five years, the small group—consisting of Temuchin, his mother, Ho'elun, three brothers, two half brothers, one sister, and one old woman—lived a hand-to-mouth existence. Most of their horses were stolen, and they struggled to feed themselves by gathering wild berries, hunting birds and other small game, and fishing in the Onon.

When Temuchin was about fourteen or fifteen years old, several things happened. First, he shot his older half brother, Bekhter, for stealing food from him and thus became the head of the family. Second, he was captured by the Tayichi'ut and held prisoner for several months before escaping. Third, he sought out his fiancée, Borte, married her, and brought her and her sable cloak back to his camp.

Borte had intended the cloak as a gift to her new mother-in-law. Temuchin, however, had other plans. He was determined to be a chief like his late father. That meant he needed a patron who would help him protect his family and gain followers.

Temuchin approached Toghrul, the head of the Kerait tribe, and reminded him that he and Yisugei had been blood brothers. "In earlier days you swore friendship with my father, Yisugei," Temuchin said. "Accordingly, you are as my own father and I bring you my wife's wedding gift." Toghrul was delighted with the present and replied: "I will reunite your scattered people. . . . I will bring back to you your straying kinsmen."

The alliance between Toghrul and Temuchin received a major test when Temuchin turned seventeen. A tribe called the Merkit wanted revenge for the fact that Yisugei had stolen Temuchin's mother, Ho'elun, from her Merkit husband some twenty years earlier. According to Mongol custom, a wrongdoing had to be accounted for, if not by the person who committed the wrong, then by his son. Accordingly, some three hundred Merkits swept down on Temuchin's camp, bent on capturing Borte. Realizing the situation, Temuchin abandoned his wife (whom he knew would not be harmed), flung himself on a horse, and raced off to Toghrul's camp to seek aid. Toghrul raised an army and appointed Temuchin's blood brother Jamuka as its leader. Temuchin himself mobilized a group of herdsmen who hoped to obtain animals and other loot if he succeeded in defeating the Merkits. He did succeed, and he and Borte were reunited.

Head of All the Mongols

After their victory, Temuchin and Jamuka became inseparable. They renewed their oath of blood brotherhood, and they and their followers formed a single group that migrated from pasture to pasture. The two young men feasted and danced together, and even shared the same blanket at night.

Temuchin and Jamuka were similar in many ways. Both were brave, shrewd, ambitious, and natural leaders. But there were differences as well. Temuchin came from a tribe of horse breeders, whereas Jamuka's tribe were sheepherders, a distinction that was very important to the Mongols. Temuchin believed the way to power lay in courting the aristocracy. Jamuka, who was of lower birth than his friend, sought the support of the common men. The differences eventually led to friction, and after eighteen months, the two parted company.

From then on, Temuchin moved steadily toward his goal of becoming head of all the Mongol tribes. He already had a reputation for being an excellent fighter. Now he became known for his generosity. He gave horses, food, and furs to individuals who joined him. He promised leadership positions and beautiful women to various chiefs. People began telling each other that "The Prince [Temuchin] dresses his people in his own clothes, he permits them to ride his own horses; this man could certainly bring peace to the tribe and rule the nation." Tales began to spread that Temuchin had been destined by Heaven to rule the world. Finally, a council of tribal chiefs elected Temuchin as their khan, or ruler. They swore to obey his orders in battle and not to meddle in his affairs in peacetime.

Temuchin now had an important title. But he was still a minority

This Persian manuscript illustration shows Genghis Khan seated on a throne as if he were a Persian king.

leader. The majority of the Mongol tribes supported Jamuka. Temuchin, however, was determined to rule over all the Mongol people. The question was how to achieve that. The answer was through organization and discipline.

In the past, the members of a tribe were not assigned to particular tasks. Each might perform any job at any given time. Now, Temuchin organized his followers in a specialized way. He made some men responsible for providing food and drink for his army. He put others in charge of training the horses, or maintaining the tent wagons, or protecting the herds. He appointed a commanding officer for each camp. And he chose a number of youths to serve as his personal bodyguard. This new organization gave him a firm foundation for pursuing his goal.

Temuchin versus Jamuka

The competition between Temuchin and Jamuka for leadership of the Mongols soon erupted into war. Jamuka launched the first attack. He took Temuchin by surprise and defeated him soundly. He then killed most of the men he had taken as prisoners, boiling seventy of them alive. The Mongols believed this method of execution prevented a person's spirit from seeking revenge. Also, the Mongols did not believe in shedding the blood of princes or generals.

After his defeat, Temuchin resettled farther south, where he continued gathering followers. Historians disagree about the events of the next several years. In 1201, however, Temuchin, together with his patron Toghrul, defeated Jamuka in battle. The victory made Toghrul's oldest son, Senggum, fearful of his own position.

Nothing was allowed to block the view from Genghis Khan's tent, which was always the first tent to go up when the Mongols made camp.

So he persuaded his father to break the alliance and attack Temuchin. Although the attack was successful, Temuchin regrouped his forces and later that year, 1203, succeeded in turning the tables. He defeated Toghrul and Senggum, and added their Kerait tribe to the ranks of his army.

The final battle between Temuchin and Jamuka took place in 1204. Once again, Temuchin was victorious, and once again, he added the defeated tribes to the ranks of his army.

Following his defeat, Jamuka hid in exile but was eventually captured and brought before Temuchin. The khan, remembering their childhood friendship, urged Jamuka to renew their oath of blood brotherhood. Jamuka refused, saying, "When I should have been a good companion, I was no companion to you. Now, my friend, you have pacified the peoples of this region and have united alien lands. The supreme throne is yours." Temuchin had no choice but to have Jamuka executed.

Two years later, the chiefs of all the Mongol tribes held a *kuriltai*, or great assembly. They elected Temuchin, then about thirty-nine years old, as Great Khan over all the Mongols. They also gave him a new title, Genghis Khan, meaning "Oceanic Ruler." And for the next twenty-one years, his armies rolled across Asia like the waves of the sea.

Genghis's War Machine

Genghis Khan's first task was turning a collection of tribes into a nation. He decided that the way to do this was by reorganizing his soldiers. Accordingly, he placed men from different tribes in the same military unit. He promoted men on the basis of their leadership skills and fighting ability rather than their tribal rank. He insisted that ordinary soldiers receive the same food as their officers. All this weakened the power of tribal leaders and strengthened the soldiers' loyalty to Genghis.

All males aged fifteen to seventy had to serve in Genghis's army. The only men exempt from military duty were doctors, priests, and undertakers.

Genghis organized his soldiers into units of ten, which were grouped into units of one hundred. These in turn were grouped into units of one thousand, which were then combined into units of ten thousand. Ten-man and hundred-man units elected their own commanders. The commanders of the larger units were appointed by Genghis Khan.

Genghis was very shrewd in his choice of unit commanders. The story is told that he once passed over a man who was both brave and strong. When challenged about his decision, Genghis replied, "This man is indeed a hero and an able fighter. And it's

The Mongol army was the most mobile army in the world until the invention of the gasoline engine.

true that he scoffs at hardship and ignores fatigue. But precisely because he assumes that every man who serves under him is like himself, he should not be in command of an army. A good commander . . . must understand what his followers feel—or he will allow his warriors to suffer and his horses to starve."

The members of a military unit were expected to act together at all times. For example, if two men in a unit of ten moved forward to attack, the rest of the unit were supposed to follow; otherwise, they were put to death. If in a group of one hundred, ten men retreated, the rest of the group were killed unless they likewise took flight. Unit members were also expected to help one another. If a soldier was captured, the rest of his unit were put to death if they failed to rescue him.

Soldiers had to remain in the unit to which they were assigned. The unit commander also had charge of the soldiers' wives, who followed behind the army and were responsible for seeing to it that their husbands were always ready for battle. A soldier's wife was expected to keep his clothes in good condition and his saddle-bags filled with food.

The Mongol army was not only well organized, it was also well trained. One way in which Genghis Khan drilled his troops was through team hunts that lasted for three months every winter. The tactics used to kill game were then transferred to the battlefield.

One such tactic was the "feint." Two or three horsemen would provoke an animal into attacking them. Then the men would gallop away, and other horsemen who had been lying in wait would attack the animal and kill it.

Another tactic was the "circle and close-in." The men would string themselves out in a long line and then ride forward, herding before them all the game they came across as they rode. When the men neared their destination, the flanks of the line, the right and left sides, would turn and ride toward each other. The game that the men had been herding were trapped.

Another asset of the Mongol army was its communication system. Commanders used black and white signal flags to instruct their troops on how and when to move. If there were natural obstructions in the way, or if the battle took place at night, the Mongols used flaming arrows instead of flags.

If the distance between several Mongol armies was too great for either flags or arrows, army commanders relied on special messengers known as "arrow riders," who rode without stopping day or night. These men actually slept in the saddle! To protect themselves against the bounding of their horses, they wrapped their heads, chests, and stomachs with tight cloth bandages. Bells on their leather belts warned people at way stations twenty-five miles apart that a messenger was approaching and needed a fresh horse. In this way, "arrow riders" took only a few days to cover distances that normally took several weeks. In addition to carrying military orders, the messengers brought Genghis Khan news about events in his empire and carried his laws to his people.

The Rule of Law

Genghis Khan's laws were eventually consolidated in a legal code commonly known as the *Yasa*. It contained both old laws the Mongols had always followed and new laws designed to help the Mongols rule their empire. There were laws against lying, spying, and interfering in other people's quarrels. There were laws requiring that all religions be treated with equal respect. There were laws about how to carry out military operations and how to conduct relations with other nations. There were laws against stealing and about the importance of returning lost property. There were even laws against alcoholism. Genghis disapproved of the excessive use of alcohol because it caused men to beggar themselves by drinking away their horses and herds. However, he was realistic. He favored moderation rather than prohibition. So a man was allowed to become drunk three times within one month before he was punished.

Genghis warned the Mongols to follow his laws without change. "If the great, the military leaders born in the future, should not adhere strictly to the law, then the power of the state will be shattered and come to an end."

In keeping with his tribal obligations, Genghis also provided for the care of Mongols who suffered ill fortune. For example, he maintained a fund for orphans whose fathers had been killed in battle. He saw to it that injured or crippled Mongols received cattle, cheese, and felt, the material used in making tents. All this helped keep his followers loyal.

To the right of Genghis Khan's tent is part of his standard of nine white yak-tails. Each yak-tail represented one of his chief commanders. Yaks, longhaired oxen, were found mostly in Mongolia's higher regions, where they often served as pack animals.

Acquiring an Empire

Soon after his election as Great Khan, Genghis began the conquests that would make him ruler of one of the largest empires the world has ever known. His first success, however, did not involve fighting. The Uighurs of west-central Asia voluntarily offered him their allegiance. Genghis accepted, and gave one of his daughters in marriage to the Uighur ruler.

Genghis's second success was against the Tanguts of Xi-Xia. Xi-Xia lay south of Mongolia (in what is now western China) and was known for the beautiful silk and wool cloth its weavers produced. Its herds were a great attraction for the Mongols, who had lost thousands of animals because of their constant fighting and, perhaps, because of climatic changes. Xi-Xia also controlled many of the oases along the Silk Road, the trade artery that ran from China to Persia (now Iran) and beyond. Silk, jade, and spices moved west over the Silk Road, while gold, horses, and glass moved east. Conquering Xi-Xia added immensely to the Mongols' wealth.

It also taught the Mongols how to attack walled cities. They learned to use ladders to scale walls. They learned to make oversized shields to protect themselves from spears and arrows that descended from above. And they learned how to demolish walls by means of catapults that hurled one-hundred-pound stones.

Conquering Northern China

This new knowledge proved invaluable to the Mongols in their next war, against the kingdom of the Jurchen (Jurchid) in northern China. The Jurchen army far outnumbered the Mongol army. Nevertheless, after three years of fighting, the Mongols managed to surround the Jurchen capital of Zhongdu (present-day Beijing). But there was no siege. Instead, the Jurchen emperor offered the Mongols a huge amount of gold, silver, and other valuables if they would withdraw. Genghis agreed.

Later that year, however, Genghis changed his mind. He learned that the Jurchen had moved their capital to the south and were assembling an army, presumably to invade Mongolia. Furious at the apparent treachery, the Mongols raced toward Zhongdu and knocked down its walls. Genghis then decided to serve up a warning to future enemies. One historian describes what took place: "Mongol horsemen rode through the streets firing flaming arrows into the wooden houses. Whole districts were burned to the ground . . . and the streets were greasy with human fat and covered with carcasses." The bones of the slaughtered formed a huge white hill in the center of the city.

The tactic of terror worked. The Koreans, who lived to the east of the Mongols, immediately sent envoys to Genghis Khan, promising to pay him a large tribute each year if his soldiers would leave them alone.

The Quarrel with the Khwarazm Shah

The Koreans were not the only ones who reacted to the destruction

Genghis Khan was able to capture walled cities with the help of Chinese and Turkish military engineers, who taught the Mongols how to use such devices as catapults, siege towers, and scaling ladders.

of Zhongdu. Another interested party was the Sultan Ala ad-Din Muhammad, better known as the Khwarazm Shah. His empire of Khwarazm, which lay west of Mongolia, was the strongest military power in Asia. It was also one of the continent's richest empires, since it contained the cities of Bukhara and Samarkand, two major stopping points along the Silk Road.

The Khwarazm Shah had contemplated conquering northern

China himself. When he learned that Genghis Khan had gotten there first, he decided that the Mongols were a threat to his power. So he sent a group of merchants from Bukhara to visit Genghis and scout out conditions at the Mongol court. Merchants in those days commonly acted as spies, reporting back on such matters as people's morale and the size and disposition of troops.

Genghis welcomed the merchants and sent them home laden with jade, gold, ivory, and other gifts for the shah. He also sent back a letter saying that after the conquests he had already made, he had no need of other lands. Instead, he suggested that he and the shah encourage trade between their empires. The shah accepted the Mongol offer of peace. But secretly he began to prepare his troops for war.

The war began later that same year, 1218. A Mongol trading caravan arrived at the city of Utrar in the eastern part of Khwarazm.

Genghis Khan encouraged trade throughout his empire by protecting merchants from robbers.

The city's governor, apparently acting on the shah's orders, killed the merchants and confiscated their goods. Genghis was furious when he learned of the incident. However, he tried to settle the matter peacefully by asking the shah to turn the governor over to him for punishment. The shah refused. Not only did he refuse, he ordered one of Genghis's envoys killed, while the other two envoys had their beards burned off and were sent home in disgrace.

That was too much for Genghis. "The Khwarazm-shah is no king, he is a bandit! If he were a king he would not have killed my merchants and my envoys. . . . Kings do not kill envoys!" Climbing to the top of a hill, Genghis spent the next three days praying to Heaven. "I was not the author of this trouble. Grant me the strength to exact vengeance." Then he came down from the hill and prepared to invade Khwarazm.

A Seven-Year War

Before starting his campaign, Genghis Khan named his successor. He passed over his oldest son, Jochi, who was suspected of being illegitimate. His son Chagadei was an excellent fighter but very arrogant, while his son Tolui, although a military genius, was cruel and mean-spirited. That left Genghis's fourth son, Ogodei, who was good-tempered, generous, and very skillful at getting people to work together. Genghis felt that these qualities would ensure the continuation of both his empire and his dynasty. So despite the fact that Ogodei liked to drink too much, Genghis designated him the next Great Khan.

Genghis issued a call to arms, and some two hundred thousand Mongols, Chinese, and Uighurs responded. The Tanguts of Xi-Xia, however, refused. If Genghis did not have enough soldiers to fight his wars, they said, then perhaps he shouldn't fight them at all! It was an insult for which the Tanguts would pay dearly in the future.

The army of the Khwarazm Shah was about twice the size of Genghis's army. So Genghis decided to split his warriors into four corps and attack Khwarazm on four fronts simultaneously. That would make the enemy believe the Mongol forces were much larger than they were. Genghis also launched a propaganda campaign. He fed forged letters to the shah, suggesting that many of the shah's nobles were ready to desert him and side with the Mongols. That made the shah unwilling to appoint an overall military commander. Instead, he spread his troops among the cities, which made them easy to defeat one by one. Genghis also fanned

Genghis Khan selects his successor from among his sons. Although Ogodei was chosen, all four brothers received territory to rule after the Great Khan's death.

the anger of the shah's subjects over his religious persecutions and heavy taxes. That lowered the people's will to resist the Mongol attack.

Genghis's army began its campaign in the spring of 1219. The second corps, led by Ogodei and Chagadei, laid siege to the city of Utrar and captured it after six months of heavy fighting. In revenge for the execution of the Mongol merchant caravan the preceding year, the Mongol forces destroyed Utrar and slaughtered almost all its inhabitants.

The third corps of Genghis's army was led by a general named Jebei, while the fourth corps was led by Jochi. These two corps moved south together and then split to attack various cities. A city escaped destruction if it surrendered without resisting. Otherwise, the Mongols razed it to the ground.

In the meantime, the first corps, led by Genghis and his senior general Subedei, headed for Bukhara. But instead of moving directly west, they followed a secret route across a desert, emerged several hundred miles behind the enemy lines, and attacked Bukhara by coming east. After killing all its defenders, the Mongols plundered the city. While they were doing so, a fire broke out. It burned the closely packed wooden houses, and what had once been a great center both of commerce and of learning was left in ruins.

From Bukhara, Genghis and Subedei headed for Samarkand, driving their prisoners before them as a human shield against enemy arrows. Samarkand, the shah's capital, was heavily fortified, and the Mongols expected a long siege. To their delighted surprise, the city's merchants and Muslim clergy offered to surrender Samarkand in exchange for their lives and protection. Five days later, the Mongols entered the city. They put its defending soldiers

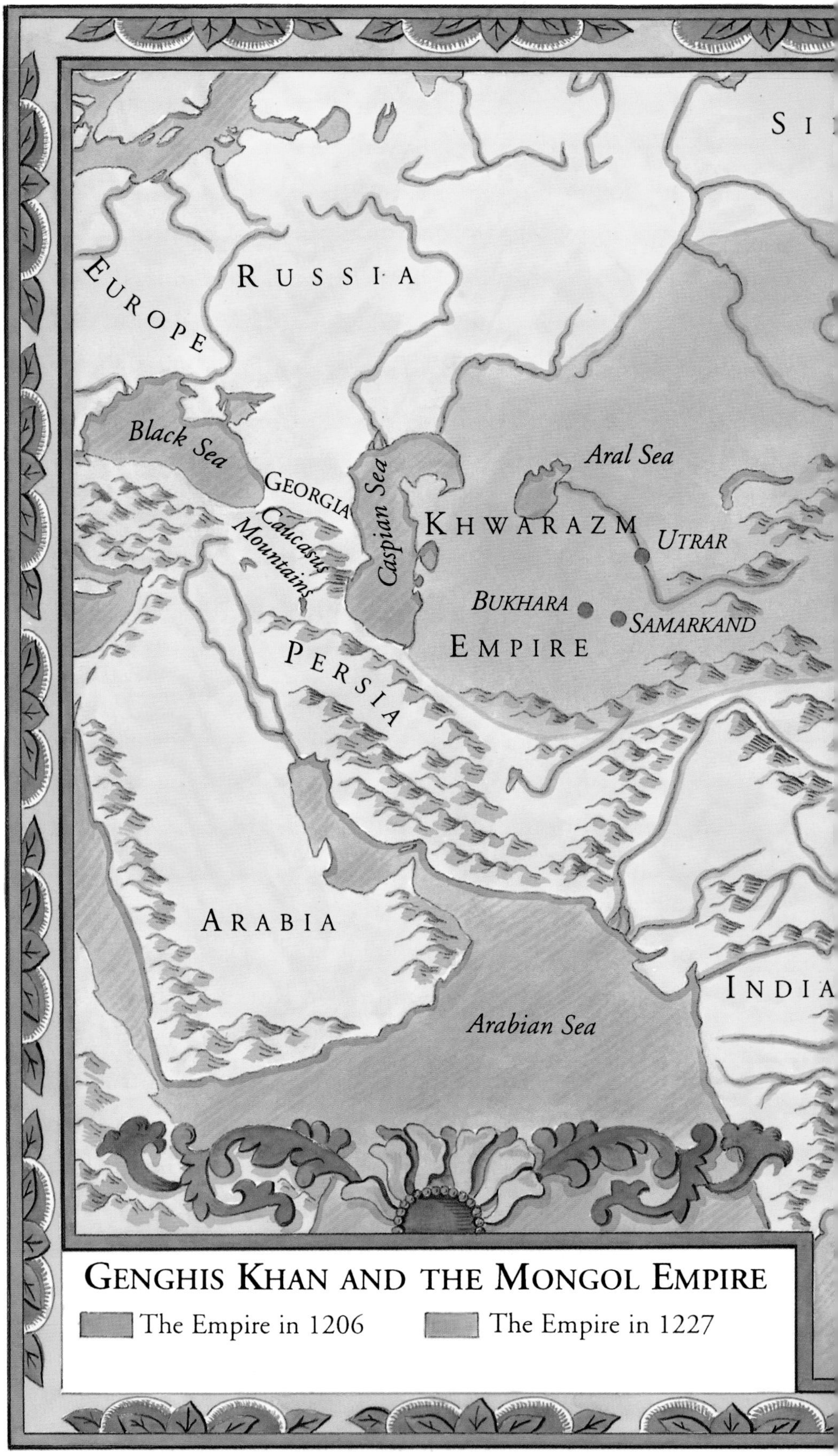

SI

SI

RUSSIA

EUROPE

Black Sea

Aral Sea

GEORGIA

KHWARAZM

Caucasus
Mountains

Caspian Sea

UTRAR

BUKHARA

SAMARKAND

EMPIRE

PERSIA

ARABIA

INDIA

Arabian Sea

GENGHIS KHAN AND THE MONGOL EMPIRE

The Empire in 1206   The Empire in 1227

I A

Mongols

Onon River

Merkits

Keraits

Tartars

Gobi Desert

Jurchen

Koreans

JAPAN

Tanguts

ZHONGDU

XI-XIA EMPIRE

rs

Hwang Ho River

PACIFIC

OCEAN

Yangtze River

SOUTHERN

SUNG EMPIRE

South China Sea

Bay of Bengal

N

800 mi

to death and deported most of its remaining inhabitants to Genghis's court in Mongolia.

Before Samarkand fell, both the Khwarazm Shah and his son, Jalal ad-Din, managed to escape from the city. Genghis sent Subedei and Jebei after the shah, while he and Tolui went after Jalal ad-Din.

The pursuit of the shah by Subedei and Jebei turned into what is probably the greatest cavalry achievement in history. Over the next three years, the Mongols rode for some eight thousand miles. First they circled the Caspian Sea, where the shah had taken refuge on a small island. When he died (probably of pneumonia) before the Mongols could capture him, Subedei and Jebei decided to see what lay farther west. They rode through Georgia, crossed the Caucasus Mountains in wintertime, and defeated a Russian army. They explored the area north of the Black Sea and for the first time met men from the West. The information they brought back was to prove invaluable some twenty years later, when the Mongols invaded Europe.

In the meantime, Genghis and Tolui chased Jalal ad-Din from one province of the Khwarazm Empire to another. They never caught him. Although defeated in all his battles except one, Jalal always managed to escape. In one instance, he rode his horse off a cliff that was supposedly fifty to seventy feet high! In the course of the pursuit, however, the Mongols devastated large sections of Asia. Crops were burned, dams demolished, and palaces and libraries reduced to rubble. Jalal became a great hero in Persian literature, but it was at the cost of tens of thousands of his people's lives.

The Final Years

Before returning to Mongolia, Genghis made arrangements for administering his empire. He had failed to do so after his conquest of northern China and, as a consequence, the Jurchen had taken back much of the land they had lost. Now Genghis appointed a series of personal representatives and installed them in the empire's cities. These representatives were responsible for collecting taxes and forwarding tribute. They were also in charge of levying troops from among the local population and organizing the messenger service.

Genghis also stationed garrisons of Mongol troops in the cities. Although the garrisons were not large, they were sufficient, since the people feared the Mongols and wanted peace.

During this period, Genghis started brooding over the fact that he was in poor health and nearing death. He had heard about a Chinese sage named Ch'ang-Ch'un, who was reputed to be three hundred years old. Genghis sent for Ch'ang-Ch'un and demanded to know the secret for a long life. The sage, who was actually in his early seventies, replied that although there were medicines to improve one's health, there were none that would keep a person from dying. Despite his disappointment, Genghis became friendly with Ch'ang-Ch'un, who gave him good advice on how nomads should govern city dwellers. The sage's ideas so impressed Genghis that he had them written down in both Mongolian and Chinese.

In 1225, Genghis finally headed back to Mongolia. With him

Genghis is depicted as an older man in this Persian miniature.

were tangible results of his victories: piles of gold, silk, and jewels; huge herds of animals; and tens of thousands of prisoners with special skills, such as astronomers, blacksmiths, falconers, physicians, scribes, and weavers. But instead of enjoying his wealth in peace, Genghis again went to war. He wanted revenge against the Tanguts of Xi-Xia for their failure to send troops to help in the war against Khwarazm.

As usual, the Mongols employed some clever techniques. They flooded cities by damming up rivers and then releasing the water all at once. During a battle on the frozen Hwang Ho (Yellow River), they tied pieces of felt underneath their horses' hooves so the animals would not slide around on the ice.

The Mongol military successes were marred, however, when Genghis was thrown from his horse during a hunt. He suffered severe internal injuries, and both his doctors and his generals suggested that he break off the campaign and return home to recuperate. Genghis refused. He would remain with his warriors.

The campaign continued. By the spring of 1227, the Mongols had conquered Xi-Xia's capital and were poised to advance into northern China. Then Genghis, still recovering from his injuries, came down with either malaria or typhus. After several months of illness, he died in August. He was about sixty years old.

Saddened by their loss, the Mongols placed Genghis's body on a cart and headed silently back to Mongolia. Along the way, they killed every living thing they met. The slaughtered people and animals were to serve Genghis in the next world.

Tradition has it that Genghis Khan was buried on the side of Mount Burkhan Kaldun, near the place where he had spent much of his youth. His grave has never been found.

Mourners surround the coffin of Genghis Khan.

Evaluating Genghis Khan

What kind of legacy did Genghis leave?

He ended the intertribal warfare that had divided the Mongols, and established peace and order on the grasslands. His conquests brought tremendous wealth to his people, while his *Yasa* greatly reduced crime. As a European traveler wrote a few years after Genghis's death: "War, strife, bodily harm or murder do not exist, robbers or thieves on a grand scale are not to be found among them, and for this reason their houses and the carts in which they store their wealth have neither locks nor bolts."

Genghis improved transportation and promoted trade throughout his empire. Among the valuable items that moved from China to Europe over his well-policed roads was gunpowder. Persian medicine, astronomy, and architecture moved in the opposite direction. Genghis was tolerant of other religions, and within his empire Buddhists, Christians, Confucians, Jews, Muslims, and Taoists "worshipped untroubled in their several ways."

Yet Genghis's conquests had devastating results in many places. Cities were looted and often destroyed, irrigation systems were smashed, and populations plummeted as people were either killed or transported to Mongolia. For years, Genghis's soldiers were always called "Mongol hordes," and history books portrayed them solely as ruthless, death-dealing barbarians. In recent years, however, scholars have acknowledged not just the brutality of Genghis's conquests, but also the fact that they brought about many social, cultural, and technological advances in much of Asia.

Genghis left a mixed legacy. Along with war and conquest, he brought changes that improved life in many parts of Asia.

PART TWO

A caravan of merchants travels along the Silk Road. The Silk Road actually was not one road but a group of ancient trade routes that connected China and Europe.

aquesta carauana es partida del unpi
de sarra panar ralcatavo :

camul

fobur

The Land

The traditional homeland of the Mongol people contained three kinds of vegetation. To the north was a band of dense forests, mostly cedar, fir, larch, and pine. To the south lay the Gobi, a great stony desert with a sandy fringe along its western border. Between the forests and the desert ran the steppe. This is a flat or gently rolling expanse of grassy plains without trees, broken here and there by fast-flowing rivers and large, salty lakes. Several mountain ranges towered to the north and west.

The climate of Mongolia varied. During the short summer, temperatures averaged 64°F but sometimes rose above 100°F. During the long winter, many of the rivers turned to solid ice, while the temperature routinely plunged to 25°F below zero. It reached as low as 50°F below zero in January, the coldest month of the year. Rainfall depended on location. The mountains were covered with snow in winter, the steppe received enough rain to maintain its cover of grass, while the desert was very dry. Winds were harsh, often blowing at sixty miles an hour.

Both the vegetation and the climate had a strong influence on the Mongolian way of life.

The sand dunes of the Gobi are often a thousand feet high. Products of the Gobi include cashmere yarn, semiprecious stones, and dinosaur bones and eggs.

Herds and Horses

When the Mongols were not at war, they lived the typical life of pastoral nomads. Their two most important possessions were their herds and their horses.

The Mongols earned their living by tending grazing animals. These included sheep, cattle, and goats, which furnished their owners with meat, milk, skins, and wool. The animals grazed in open pastures. When a pasture ran out of grass, the herds were moved to a fresh pasture. In general, the migration was seasonal. The herds moved from high, flat, open summer pastures to more sheltered winter pastures in low-lying valleys. The migrations covered anywhere from a few miles to several hundred miles, and sometimes took a month or more to complete.

The movement of the herds determined the seasonality of work. Springtime was the busiest time of the year. People had to help the animals with difficult births and make sure that the newborn kids and lambs were nursing properly. Late spring meant shearing the sheep for their wool and combing the cashmere goats for their underwool.

Then came the migration to summer pastures. With abundant food available, people could relax and enjoy sports events and festivals.

As autumn approached, the people would gather for the migration to winter pastures. There they would repair their equipment and check their food supplies. This included killing sheep and freezing the mutton by burying it in the ground.

Winter was the most difficult time of the year. People struggled to keep their animals alive on the open range and huddled inside their tents, trying to keep warm.

The Mongols valued their horses for several reasons. The animals provided an excellent means of transportation. In addition, those with horses were able to control larger herds of animals than herders working on foot and, therefore, could become richer. Horses also enabled the Mongols to defend their pastures and their migration routes against attack. Hunting from horseback was easier than hunting on foot. And horsemen could sweep down on settled communities and raid them for such items as cloth, coffee, grain, metal, salt, sugar, tea, and often slaves.

Mongolian horses were thickset and sturdy, with broad foreheads

The pole used to lasso horses was about thirty feet long and was made of either bamboo or willow.

and dense coats. Their legs were too short to cover much distance by walking, while cantering over the steppe was too tiring. So, most of the time, Mongols rode their horses at a rapid trot. The riders either relaxed limply in the saddle or rose in the stirrups and swayed with the motion of the horse. Genghis Khan's cavalry was able to cover up to eighty miles a day when its horses were well rested and in good condition after summer feeding.

Mongolian horses were broken and ridden hard from the time they were born until they reached the age of two. They spent the next three years out to pasture, where they roamed wild in herds of ten thousand or more. Then they were ridden again. Whenever a Mongol needed another horse, he would take a long, springy pole with a noose attached to one end and capture an animal by throwing the noose over its head.

A Portable House

Genghis Khan often referred to the Mongols as the "people who live in felt tents." The typical Mongolian house was a round portable tent known as a ger. Its frame consisted of sections of latticework, or crossed wooden strips. The sections were tied together to form a circular shape. The more sections of latticework, the larger the ger. However, a typical ger measured about fifteen feet in diameter. There was space between two sections of latticework for a wooden door frame. The door frame faced south, which the Mongols considered the lucky direction, especially since the prevailing cold winds blew from the north. Wooden poles and a round, wooden roof wheel formed a domed ceiling.

Once the ger's frame was completed, the Mongols covered it with several layers of thick felt, which they made by matting wool. They coated the felt with tallow to make it waterproof. A dangling felt flap formed the door. The roof wheel was left open to let in light and air and to allow smoke to escape. It could be closed, however, by a felt flap that was controlled by cords from the ground. Planking, felt, or furs covered the ger's floor.

The Mongols placed a square-shaped hearth directly under the roof wheel. (Children collected animal droppings for fuel.) They lined the walls of the ger with wooden beds and storage chests. These were carved and decorated with painted designs in such colors as red, orange, and yellow. Meat and weapons were suspended

Probably a majority of Mongolians today still live in gers. An iron stove has replaced the hearth, with the stovepipe coming out through the roof. Doors are now made of wood rather than felt and are brightly painted.

on horns that were attached to the latticework. The head of the household always sat facing the ger's door. Women sat to the east, men to the west.

To the Mongols, the ger was a miniature universe. The domed ceiling stood for Heaven, while the square-shaped hearth stood for the earth. Accordingly, they followed strict rules about using a ger. The felt door covering had to be lifted from the right side, and it was considered very rude to step on the bottom of the door frame or to burn rubbish in the hearth.

It took only about two hours to assemble or disassemble a ger. Its six-hundred-pound weight could easily be carried in an oxcart over rocky terrain or by pack camel over sand or grass. A ger was well ventilated in summer, warm and snug in winter, strong enough to stand up against high winds, and proof against the heaviest rain and snow. It was a perfect house for a nomadic people.

A Simple Diet

The Mongolian diet was very simple: essentially, it consisted of meat and tea. The meat was usually mutton from sheep, which the Mongols boiled in a stew. Sometimes they hunted small game, such as mice and marmots, or larger game, such as wolves, foxes, and rabbits. They also ate "camel if necessary, horseflesh under duress," except if the horse had been ridden in battle. Most of the time, however, boiled mutton was their staple food. Family members ate from a common pot. They stored leftovers in a leather bag.

Mongols usually drank between twenty and thirty cups of tea a day. They often mixed the tea with butter and roasted barley. They also drank vast quantities of mare's milk, which was usually fermented into a mildly alcoholic beverage known as koumiss. Sometimes they turned the milk into curds, yogurt, or cheese.

Summers in Mongolia are too short to grow green vegetables. In any event, nomadic herders seldom stay in one place long enough to plant and harvest a garden. Accordingly, the only additions to the Mongolian diet were whatever people could gather wild. This included juniper berries and hazelnuts, garlic and onions, apples, cherries, and the roots of certain grasses. It also included mushrooms, some of which measured as much as fifteen inches in diameter.

Clothing and Jewelry

Mongol men and women wore similar clothing. The most common style consisted of a pair of trousers and a long robe called a *del* that was slit along both sides to make riding on horseback easy. The robe fastened on the right and had a stand-up collar. Men's robes also had a cloth belt folded several times around the waist. A winter *del* was made of sheepskin; a summer robe, of cotton.

Both men and women wore high leather boots with slightly turned-up toes. The boots were often tooled or decorated with silk, metal, or bits of colored leather. Inside the boots were socks made of cloth or felt. In winter, both men and women wore leather or felt hats trimmed with fur. Their summer hats were made of plush. Since different Mongol tribes wore hats of different shapes, it was easy to tell which tribe a person belonged to.

Mongols seldom washed their clothes. They believed that running water was a living spirit. Accordingly, they considered it a sin to pollute the water by using it to wash off dirt. Occasionally, they washed their clothes in meat broth. But usually they simply wore their clothes without washing until the garments fell apart.

As is the case in most nomadic societies, Mongols stored their wealth in the form of jewelry. Men decorated their saddles with silk and velvet appliqué, silk tassels, silver fittings, and silver- or

A Mongol archer and his horse are both adorned with finery.

brass-plated iron stirrups carved into designs such as dragons' heads. Leather scabbards trimmed with silver, coral, and turquoise dangled from their belts. Women slung ropes of silver, coral, and turquoise around their necks and attached long jeweled pendants to their headgear.

Battle Gear

Mongol soldiers were well equipped when they rode into battle. Next to their bodies, they wore a tightly woven silk undershirt. This was to protect them if they were struck by an arrow. Although an arrow might penetrate a soldier's armor, it would not pierce the silk but would bring the silk with it into the body. It was then possible to remove the arrow by pulling gently on the silk. This left only a small wound, whereas pulling an arrow directly out of one's body would leave a much larger wound. The silk also helped to protect the wound against infection.

Over his undershirt, a Mongol soldier wore a blue or brown tunic that was lined with fur in winter. He also wore blue or gray trousers that, like the tunic, were lined with fur in winter. If he were part of the light cavalry, whose main task was shooting arrows at the enemy, he covered his tunic with a leather vest. If he were part of the heavy cavalry that engaged in hand-to-hand combat, he wore a coat of mail and a vest of oxhide or leather-covered iron scales. The light cavalry wore leather helmets; the heavy cavalry, iron helmets.

Every soldier carried a leather-covered wicker shield, one long-range bow, one short-range bow, and two quivers containing at least sixty arrows. The arrows served a variety of purposes. There were arrows that could pierce armor. There were arrows that whistled in flight and were used for signaling and identifying

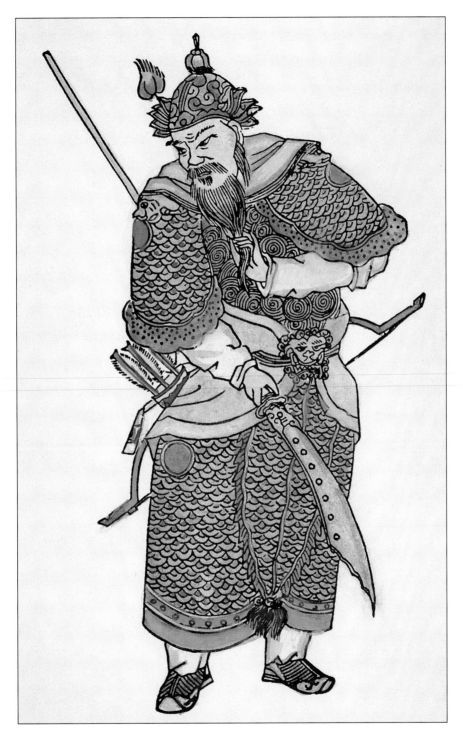

A Mongol warrior as depicted by a thirteenth-century Chinese artist

targets. There were incendiary arrows that set fire to their targets. And there were arrows tipped with tiny grenades that exploded on contact. The Mongols were such skillful archers that they were able to shoot in any direction while galloping at full speed.

In addition to bows and arrows, light cavalry soldiers were armed with a small sword and two or three javelins, or short spears. Heavy cavalry soldiers carried a curved sword called a scimitar, a battle-ax, and a twelve-foot lance with a hook at the end for unseating enemy horsemen.

Each Mongol soldier also carried a saddlebag. Because it was made from a cow's stomach, it was inflatable and waterproof. So, in addition to carrying food, clothing, cooking pots, and such items as a needle and thread, it served as a sort of life jacket when the army crossed a river.

Each Mongol soldier was equipped with four or five horses. When one horse tired, the soldier simply changed mounts and continued riding. This enabled the Mongol cavalry to continue moving forward for days at a time and to cover much greater distances much more rapidly than their opponents.

Family Life

Mongol babies were formally named three days after they were born. They usually received a single name, such as Hulegu for a boy, Toregene for a girl. The naming was celebrated by a feast at which relatives brought gifts to the mother and child.

Mongol children received their first haircut when they were three years old. Once again, the event was celebrated by a feast. The oldest relative of the child cut the first lock of hair and gave the child a gift. Then the other relatives did the same. The child's mother collected the hair clippings in a silk scarf and later sewed the scarf inside the child's pillow.

Inside the ger of a Mongol family today

Unless a man kidnapped his future wife, marriages were arranged by the parents of the bride and groom. The wedding celebration lasted for three days and included several rounds of gift giving and feasting. Although wealthier Mongol men had several wives, the first one was the most important. Only her children were considered their father's heirs.

Women in general played a major role in Mongolian society. If the men were away on military campaigns or for other reasons, the women not only tended and milked the herds but also governed the clan. They always cared for the children, made people's clothes, drove the oxcarts when the clan moved, and sewed the felt tents. They also prepared most of the meals. The wives of chieftains often gave their husbands advice and sometimes accompanied them into battle. After a fight was over, the women ranged over the battlefield collecting arrows and killing the enemy wounded.

Nevertheless, wives were expected to obey their husbands. Men were always served food first. Women ate only after the men had finished their meal.

When Mongols died, they were buried, together with valuable possessions, in a spot they had liked when they were alive. The graves of chieftains were kept secret. Sometimes the burial took place at night, and horses were driven over the grave site to destroy all evidence of digging. At other times the slaves who had helped with the burial were killed to prevent their revealing the grave's location. In contrast, the graves of ordinary Mongols were not hidden. A pole was placed on top, and the skin of the dead person's horse was hung on it.

Sports and Games

All Mongol men were expected to be skilled in the "three manly sports" of archery, horse racing, and wrestling. Events in these sports highlighted every holiday celebration, and champions won glory not only for themselves but also for their tribe.

Mongol archers competed both from a standing position and from horseback. They used a double-curved bow that was made of several different materials, including wood, bamboo, horn, and sinew. A glue made from boiled fish skin held the materials together. The bow was strong and flexible enough to drive an arrow some 250 yards. An archer named Isuke once hit the target from a distance of 300 yards. The feat so impressed Genghis Khan that he had a stone tablet erected in Isuke's honor.

Since all Mongols learned to ride when they learned to walk, horse races tested the horse rather than the rider. The races were run cross-country, and the length of the course varied from nine miles for two-year-old horses to as much as twenty miles for adult animals.

Wrestling was perhaps the most distinctive of the "three manly sports." Contestants wore heavy leather boots, tight-fitting trunks, and a short embroidered jacket that covered the back and the arms but left the chest bare. Upon entering the ring, each wrestler adopted a stance designed to resemble the movement of the mythical Garuda bird. They extended their arms to the side and

Polo, a game played on horseback, was popular among the Mongols. It probably started in Persia.

moved them up and down like the wings of a bird in flight. Then they grabbed each other's jackets, each man trying to force the other to touch the ground with his elbow and knee. When the match was over, the loser knelt, while the victor performed a slow-motion "eagle dance," holding his arms above his head.

Another favorite sport of the Mongols was falconry, or hunting by means of trained birds such as eagles, falcons, and hawks. A Mongol carried his hunting bird on his right hand. A leather thong was looped around the bird's neck and hung down the middle of its chest. When the Mongol cast his bird at its prey, he pulled on the leather thong with his left hand. This kept the bird's head and chest at a downward angle so that the wind could not carry it up or blow it backward. When the bird was not hunting, its head was covered by a hood.

In winter, a favorite Mongol pastime was kicking a circular disk made from camel or ox bone around an ice field. Players gained points depending on where the disk stopped. The Mongols also enjoyed playing chess, which had been introduced from India by way of Persia. The rules were similar to those used in the West but some of the pieces were different. For example, the Mongols used a camel instead of a bishop, and a dog instead of a queen.

The Arts

Being a nomadic people, the Mongols emphasized portable arts. These included oral literature, music, and dance.

Poetry was an important part of oral literature. Professional bards recited epic poems at special events. People used poetic blessings in their everyday conversation. For example, if you saw a woman embroidering, you might say: "May thy hand be skillful and thy work a success." People used similar blessings when welcoming guests or starting out on a journey.

The Mongols were also extremely fond of folktales, which they recited at festivals and in marketplaces. The folktales dealt with topics ranging from romance to the supernatural. There were stories about the deeds of famous heroes, and stories about wandering monks and the tricks they played on unsuspecting people.

The oldest Mongolian musical instrument was the wooden *morin khuur*, or horse-head fiddle, so-called because there was a horse head carved at the instrument's top. It had a leather sounding board and two strings that were played with a wood-and-horsehair bow. Every Mongol man was expected to know how to play the *morin khuur*, just as he was expected to be skilled in the "three manly sports."

The Mongols had many legends about the origin of the *morin khuur*. One such legend tells about a Mongol chieftain who had to get to a far-off camp within twenty-four hours. His horse

Genghis Khan and his court enjoy a folktale. Although anybody could become a storyteller, the most common storytellers were older people. Sometimes they accompanied themselves on a musical instrument.

reached the destination in time but was so exhausted that it collapsed and died. The sorrowing chieftain thereupon cut off the animal's head, attached it to the top of a fiddle, and spent the rest of his life playing the instrument and singing about his horse.

The Mongols loved to sing. They sang herding songs to call back animals that had strayed from the herd. They sang work songs while pitching camp. They sang songs in praise of famous horses or beautiful spots in the Mongolian landscape. They sang songs at the start of all important events, especially sports competitions.

A distinctive form of Mongolian singing was called *hoomi* or *khoomei*, which means "harmonic singing" or "split-tone singing." It was performed only by men, since it required very strong abdominal and throat muscles. The singer would sing a constant bass note using his chest and diaphragm. At the same time, he would weave a melody of high notes and whistles using his throat and nasal passages. The result sounded like two or three people singing together.

Mongolian dance was of two kinds. Group dances were performed outdoors by groups of men, of women, or of couples. Individual dances were performed inside a ger by a woman. The dancer would sit or kneel on the ground and move her body only from the waist up.

Religious Beliefs

The original religion of the Mongols was shamanism, a kind of nature worship. The Mongols believed that the sky, the sun and moon, great lakes and rivers, and high mountains were all inhabited by spirits. The supreme spirit was Tengri, or the Eternal Blue Heaven, who lived in the sky. The Mongols worshiped the spirits with music, masked dances, and animal sacrifices. The Mongols also maintained *ovoos* as a sign of respect to the spirits. An *ovoo* consisted of a pile of rocks or the branch of a large tree. A Mongol would either add a rock to the pile as an offering and walk clockwise around it, or would tie a strip of cloth to the tree branch. The cloth was colored blue, the Mongolian sacred color.

Male religious leaders were called shamans; female religious leaders were known as shamankas. When they went into a trance, they were supposed to be able to communicate with the spirits on behalf of the Mongol people. They officiated at major festivals, such as the First Mare's Milk Festival in May. At this festival, white mares were blessed and people offered the spirits the first koumiss of the season. Shamans and shamankas interpreted people's dreams. They served as healers when a person fell ill. When someone died, they carried the person's belongings between two fires to purify them of evil.

Shamans and shamankas gave advice on matters ranging from when to go to war to what the best place was to set up camp.

Genghis Khan often went to a mountaintop before the start of a campaign in order to pray for Heaven's assistance.

They predicted eclipses of the sun and moon. During an eclipse, people beat on drums and tambourines to scare off the evil spirits that had covered the sun or moon. The end of the eclipse was the signal for a great feast of celebration. The Mongols also believed that shamans and shamankas could influence the weather.

As Genghis Khan's armies spread across Asia, they learned about many different religions. Of these, the one that became increasingly important to the Mongols was Lamaism. This is a form of Buddhism that developed in Tibet. Lamaism teaches the Buddhist belief that meditation and good deeds, combined with the help of various saints, free a person from the need to be reborn over and over into a world of suffering. Lamaism also emphasizes the study of religious texts and the use of paintings and statues to show the soul's struggle against evil.

By the 1500s, Lamaism had become the national religion of the Mongol people. Beautifully decorated stone monasteries were built in Tibetan style. They stood several stories high, had elaborately carved doors, and were topped with tile roofs that curved up at the sides. The monasteries usually contained extensive libraries and served as universities where monks studied astronomy, mathematics, and medicine.

At least one son in each Mongol family was encouraged to become a monk. Some women became nuns. The chief monk of a monastery was known as a lama, while the head of Lamaism in Mongolia was known as the grand lama. (The greatest grand lama is the Dalai Lama of Tibet.) Mongols believed that each lama was the physical reincarnation of his predecessor.

The Mongo.

PART THREE

The lion is considered one of the Four Strong Animals of Mongolian folktales. The other three are the dragon, the elephant, and the Garuda bird. Many Mongolian place-names include the word *arslan*, "lion." Although no lions are to be found in Mongolia today, they may have been common centuries ago, when the climate was warmer.

The oldest Mongolian book is *The Secret History of the Mongols*. It was probably written down in the middle of the thirteenth century. Only members of the royal family, it seems, or, at most, members of the Mongol nobility, were allowed to read it. The original manuscript has not yet been located. We know the text of *The Secret History* from a Chinese translation.

The following excerpt about Alan the Fair, an ancestor of Genghis Khan, deals with the importance of the family in Mongolian society:

> *One day in the spring,*
> *while boiling a soup from dried mutton,*
> *Alan the Fair assembled her five sons together.*
> *She seated them all in a row,*
> *gave them each the shaft of an arrow*
> *and said to them: "Break it!"*
> *A single arrow shaft,*
> *it took no great strength to break it,*
> *and each of them broke it and tossed it away.*
> *Then she bound together five shafts in a bundle,*
> *and giving the bundle to each in his turn,*
> *said to each of them: "Break it!"*
> *Each of the brothers held the five bound together*
> *and no one could break them. . . .*

Then Alan the Fair spoke to her five sons and gave
them this advice:

"You five were all born from one womb.
If, like the five single arrows that you held
you separate yourselves, each going alone,
then each of you can be broken by anyone.
If you are drawn together by a singular purpose
bound like the five shafts in a bundle
how can anyone break you?"

The following folktale describes how storytelling supposedly
began among the Mongol people:

A long, long time ago, the terrible Black Plague
descended on Central Asia and began its assault on the
people of Mongolia. Thousands, young and old, died a
quick but painful death; those caught in the plague's
deadly clutches had no chance of surviving. Men and
women who remained healthy tried to save their lives.
Fleeing in panic, they cried out to each other:
"We must try to escape! Fate will decide the Destiny of
the suffering!"
Among the sick was a ten-year-old boy called Tarvaa.
For days Tarvaa's body battled the forces of Death, but

finally, weak and feverish, the young man lost all aware-
ness of this world.

Tarvaa's spirit thought that young Tarvaa had died. It
rose up out of the boy's body and began the sad journey to
the Underworld. After many difficulties, the spirit of
Tarvaa arrived before the portal of the Kingdom of the
Underworld and was led to the presence of its Great Khan.

The Khan was most surprised to see such a young spirit.
He asked sternly, "Why did you leave your body while it
was still alive? Why are you here in my Kingdom?"

Trembling with fright, the spirit replied, "Begging your
pardon, Great Khan, but all my family and all my friends
who remained in that World stood over my body and said
I was dead. Then they ran away. I did not wait for the ter-
rible last moment, but simply left on my journey to you."

The Khan was touched by the simplicity and honesty of
Tarvaa's spirit. He told the spirit gently, "Young spirit,
your Time has not yet come. You do not belong here. You
must return to your master. But before you set out on your
long journey home, I will grant you one gift. You may
choose and take back with you anything from my King-
dom that you desire."

It was only then that the spirit of Tarvaa looked about
him. As far as his eye could see in the dim light of the
Kingdom of the Underworld were every Pleasure and
every Pain to be had in life: Wealth and Poverty, Good
Fortune and Bad, Happiness and Sadness, Music and
Song, Rich Food and Clothing, Amusement and Laughter,
Ballads and Dance, and many, many other temptations,
both good and bad.

The spirit of Tarvaa wandered among all these wondrous

Listening to stories was a favorite pastime among the Mongols.

treasures for some time. It looked to the right, then to the left, but selected nothing. Only after a long search did it finally stop and stare: it had spied the one thing that Tarvaa was to value most in life.

Hesitating, the spirit pointed to something deep in the shadows, then looked back questioningly in the direction of the Khan. The Great Khan nodded his consent with a fatherly smile.

This is how the gift of Tales and Legends was bestowed upon the spirit of Tarvaa.

The Khan then instructed the spirit, "Now return home

*at once. Use this gift well in Life, and do not come here
again until you have been called!"*

*After days and nights, the spirit finally reached the
body of Tarvaa. To its distress, it found that a crow had
dug out Tarvaa's eyes in its absence. Though sad and
frightened by the terrible condition of its now sightless
body, the spirit did not dare disobey the orders of the Khan.
Silently, it slipped back into the boy's still-sleeping flesh.*

*Young Tarvaa recovered from the fearsome Black
Plague and, though blind, lived to be an old, old man.
Throughout his long life, Tarvaa would travel to the far
corners of the Mongol lands recounting wonderful Tales
and Legends to his people. They were stories not only from
his own country, but also delightful tales that he learned
from faraway lands.*

*In this way, Blind Tarvaa, known and loved by Mongo-
lians as the greatest storyteller of all time, used well the
gift bestowed upon his spirit by the Great Khan of the
Kingdom of the Underworld.*

Many Mongolian folktales have to do with animals. The animals
actually represent people, and different animals represent different
human qualities:

*Once, a long time ago, a terrible battle broke out between
the Birds and the Beasts of this Earth. No one remembers
any more what caused this battle to start, but the fighting*

was so ferocious that the whole earth shook and the land was covered with broken feathers, bloody hair, and the bodies of fallen creatures.

On one side of the battle swarmed the animals of the air. All the birds, great and small, were massed in the heavens, from the most powerful eagle, sharp-eyed hawk, and swift falcon to the tiniest finch and fragile sparrow. Opposing the birds were formidable adversaries: the kingly lion, menacing tiger, mighty stag, massive bear, and all the other beasts of the land.

The only animal in the whole world that did not choose sides in this war was the Bat. As a mouse with wings or a birdy beast, the Bat gambled on its dual nature, waiting to see which side would win. In this way, when the time came, it could claim victory with the conquering army.

When it looked as though the birds of the air were gaining the advantage, the Bat would become like a bird, flap its wings and screech:

"I'm a bird, too! I'll peck at the beasts below, pierce their skins, and dig my sharp talons into their flesh! Forward to battle, birds!"

But when the tide of the great battle shifted, and suddenly it seemed as though the beasts would win, the Bat would hide its wings and flash its mouselike grin. Baring its sharp teeth, it would bark:

"Beware! I am a dangerous Beast! C'mon beasts! Let's attack the birds and bite them till they fall from the sky! Hooray for the beasts!"

As the battle raged on and on, both the birds and the beasts displayed courage in their terrible fight, never ceasing for a moment to give their best for the sake of their cause. After many weeks of struggle, however, it became clear to everyone that both sides were evenly matched, that neither side would ever be able to overcome the other. And so the birds and the beasts agreed to cease fighting. They declared a truce.

In the quiet that followed, both armies counted their dead, collected their wounded, and called out the names of their brothers, sisters, and friends who might not have perished on the battlefield.

No one called the name of the Bat. No one wanted the one who had darted from one camp to the other throughout the long war, not knowing where it belonged, telling false things to each army in turn.

The animals had seen it fighting like this, first on one side, then on the other side of the battlefield. They were angry.

Neither the birds nor the beasts would now, or ever, agree to claim the Bat as one of their own. Instead, for its disloyalty, they banished the Bat from their midst.

The sorry Bat, a traitor to both birds and beasts, was now ashamed of its behavior during the feud. It curled up its mousy body and took flight. Seeking out a remote corner of the world, it entered the recesses of Mother Earth and concealed itself in her black and silent caves, venturing out only at night in search of food.

From that day, the Bat has made its home in the dark, wrapped against the dampness in its leathery cloak, living out the life of a lonely outcast.

Note the dragon and the fox that accompany this Mongol horseman.

Another type of Mongolian folktale has to do with someone who becomes a hero in spite of himself. Among the most famous folktales of this sort is *The Khan's Daughter*. It is the story of a simple shepherd named Mongke who must pass three tests in order to marry Borte, the khan's beautiful daughter. In the following excerpt, Mongke faces his second test:

> The Khan's scouts had brought word that the enemy was invading. . . . The Khan's wife said, "Our daughter's husband must not only be strong, but he must be brave. Let him drive the enemy from our land."
>
> Though he was even more afraid this time, Mongke sighed. "Just point the way."

So the Khan gave some horsemen to Mongke to lead in advance of the Khan's own army. And Mongke led his little band across the plains until they reached a wooded hill where they decided to rest.

Suddenly the ground shook beneath them, and a scout galloped back. "Our enemies are coming—and there are thousands of them."

Mongke nervously climbed onto his horse. "A dozen or a thousand, we'll drive them away like sheep."

However, his men grumbled, "He knows more about herding than fighting. If we follow this shepherd, we will surely die."

So while his men retreated, Mongke galloped forward—straight into a young sapling. He became so entangled with its branches that he uprooted the entire tree in his mad dash.

When the enemy saw the green-haired warrior plunge out of the woods, they stared. "One . . . five . . . I can't count all of his arms," one soldier said.

Their Khan shook with fear. "It must be one of the seven demons!"

In a panic, they fled, leaving their pack animals behind.

Mongke returned leading the long train of animals loaded down with his spoils. The Khan was amazed to see him, for Mongke's own men had reported that he had died.

Then the Khan and the people could not praise Mongke enough, and even the Khan's wife had to admit that he had proved himself worthy.

The Mongols used proverbs as well as folktales to teach people the right way to behave:

Plant only one seed of virtue;
Much fruit will be harvested.

The sun illuminates the world;
Knowledge illuminates a man.

If you've begun—finish.
If you've sought—find.

Even the largest tree cannot escape
the axe;
Even a good man is not above the law.

A horse released can be caught
again.
A word released cannot.

If you fear death, there's no point in
living.

No desire—no energy.

Once your good name is lost, you can
never destroy your evil reputation.

Strong medicine is bitter in the
mouth, but cures illness.
Harsh words are unpleasant to the
ear, but bring benefit.

The wise man tries once:
The fool twice.

When one knows a trade there is no
old age.

If you have a tail, wag it;
If you have a mind, use it.

With friends you are as broad as the
steppe. Without them you are as
narrow as the palm of your hand.

Happy is he who often has guests;
cheerful is the home near which
stand the horses of visitors.

Genghis Khan's instructions to his army chiefs resemble Mongolian proverbs in several ways. They are short, and they use animals to make their point:

When in contact with others you
must be more gentle than a small
calf, but on a campaign more fero-
cious than a terrible eagle.

When in the company of friends be
more gentle than a black calf, but
when joined in battle be as merci-
less than the black falcon.

Glossary

bard: A poet and singer.

curds: Milk that has turned sour and become thick.

disposition: Arrangement.

dowry: The money or property that a bride brings to her husband at marriage.

dynasty: A series of rulers from the same family.

envoy: A ruler's representative in another country.

epic: A long poem that tells of the adventures of heroes in legend or history.

exile: Far away, often out of the country.

khan: The Mongol ruler.

manuscript: A book that is written out, illustrated, and bound by hand.

pastoral nomads: People who wander from one pasture to another, with their animal herds.

patron: A person, especially one who is rich or powerful, who supports another person or cause.

propaganda: Ideas or information deliberately spread to influence the thinking of people; very often, propaganda is not completely true.

reincarnation: The rebirth of the soul in a new body.

sable: A small animal with very soft, dark fur.

sage: A wise and experienced person.

scabbard: A case for a sword.

shah: The Persian king.

staple food: The main or most important food of a country.

sultan: The king of certain Asian countries.

tribute: The forced payment of money or property.

For Further Reading

Brill, Marlene Targ. *Mongolia*. Chicago: Children's Press, 1992.
Hull, Mary. *The Mongol Empire*. San Diego: Lucent Books, 1998.
Humphrey, Judy. *Genghis Khan*. New York: Chelsea House, 1987.
Major, John S. *The Land and People of Mongolia*. New York: J.B. Lippincott, 1990.
Metternich, Hilary Roe. *Mongolian Folktales*. Boulder, CO: Avery Press, 1996.
Yep, Laurence. *The Khan's Daughter*. New York: Scholastic Press, 1997.

ON-LINE INFORMATION*
http://www.asianart.com/mongolia/index.html
    This site displays images of Mongolian art from an exhibit presented by the Asian Art Museum. Informative background information is also included.
http://www.indiana.edu/~mongsoc/mongolia.html
    An interesting site that offers images and information about Mongolian history and culture.
http://www.pma.edmonton.ab.ca/vexhibit/genghis/intro.htm
    A "virtual" exhibit of artifacts from around the time of Genghis Khan.

*Websites change from time to time. For additional on-line information, check with the media specialist at your local library.

Bibliography

Brent, Peter. *Genghis Khan*. New York: McGraw-Hill, 1976.
Brill, Marlene Targ. *Mongolia*. Chicago: Children's Press, 1992.
Chambers, James. *The Devil's Horsemen*. New York: Atheneum, 1985.

Hull, Mary. *The Mongol Empire*. San Diego: Lucent Books, 1998.

Humphrey, Judy. *Genghis Khan*. New York: Chelsea House, 1987.

Kahn, Paul. *The Secret History of the Mongols*. San Francisco: North Point Press, 1984.

Krueger, John R., ed. *Mongolian Folktales, Stories and Proverbs*. Bloomington, IN: The Mongolia Society, 1967.

Major, John S. *The Land and People of Mongolia*. New York: J.B. Lippincott, 1990.

Metternich, Hilary Roe. *Mongolian Folktales*. Boulder, CO: Avery Press, 1996.

Ratchnevsky, Paul. *Genghis Khan: His Life and Legacy*. Cambridge, MA: Basil Blackwell, 1992.

Severin, Tim. *In Search of Genghis Khan*. New York: Atheneum, 1992.

Yep, Laurence. *The Khan's Daughter*. New York: Scholastic Press, 1997.

Notes

Part One: The Road to Empire

Page 11. "In earlier days": Ratchnevsky, *Genghis Khan*, p. 33.

Page 11. "I will reunite": Brent, *Genghis Khan*, p. 19.

Page 12. "The Prince [Temuchin]": Ratchnevsky, *Genghis Khan*, p. 40.

Page 15. "When I should have been": Ratchnevsky, *Genghis Khan*, p. 87.

Page 17. "This man is indeed a hero": Humphrey, *Genghis Khan*, p. 63.

Page 21. "If the great, the military leaders": Ratchnevsky, *Genghis Khan*, p. 187.

Page 24. "Mongol horsemen rode": Hull, *The Mongol Empire*, p. 48.

Page 27. "The Khwarazm-shah": Ratchnevsky, *Genghis Khan*, p. 123.

Page 27. "I was not the author": Hull, *The Mongol Empire*, p . 50.

Page 36. "War, strife, bodily harm": Ratchnevsky, *Genghis Khan*, p. 205.

Page 36. "worshipped untroubled": Brent, *Genghis Khan*, p. 105.

Part Two: Everyday Life in Mongolia

Page 45. "people who live in felt tents": Major, *The Land and People of Mongolia*, p. 3.

Page 47. "camel if necessary": Severin, *In Search of Genghis Khan*, p. 52.

Page 58. "May thy hand": Major, *The Land and People of Mongolia*, p. 143.

Part Three: The Mongols in Their Own Words

Page 66. "One day in the spring": Kahn, *The Secret History of the Mongols*, pp. 5–7.

Page 67. "A long, long time ago": Metternich, *Mongolian Folktales*, pp. 33–34.

Page 70. "Once, a long time ago": Metternich, *Mongolian Folktales*, pp. 65–66.

Page 73. "The Khan's scouts": Yep, *The Khan's Daughter*, unpaged.

Page 75. "Plant only one seed": Krueger, *Mongolian Folktales, Stories and Proverbs*, pp. 63–80, and Brill, *Mongolia*, pp. 81 and 94.

Page 75. "When in contact": Brill, *Mongolia*, p. 86.

Index

Page numbers for illustrations are in **boldface**